MW01536975

Memories of You

A Healing Journey Through the Garden of Grief

By
William G. Ladewig, Esq
&
Paula vW. Dáil, PhD

Copyright © 2009 William G. Ladewig, Esq & Paula vW. Dáil, PhD
All rights reserved.

ISBN: 1-4392-6548-8
ISBN-13: 9781439265482

This Book Is a Reflection of
Someone Special Who Came into My Life
and Is Dedicated to Remembering

_____

Name

(Insert photo)

By

_____

Your name

_____

Date

Nature gives to every time and season some beauties of its own; and from morning to night, as from the cradle to the grave, it is but succession of changes so gentle and easy that we can scarcely mark their progress.

Charles Dickens

This Book Is Being Created

to Preserve the Memory of

Someone Dear to Your Heart

Who Came into Your Life and Is Now Gone.

Someone You Never Want to Forget

and You Want

to Help Others Remember.

Those we have held in our arms, even for a little while,
We hold in our hearts forever...

Introduction

Great grief is a divine and terrible radiance which transfigures even the wretched.

– Victor *Hugo: Les Misérables* V.xiii

If you have this book in your hands, it is because you are grieving the loss of someone dear to your heart.

For some of you, the loss is as close and personal as the loss of a spouse or a child. For others, it is a more distant relative or a friend who holds a special place in your heart. Regardless, losing a loved one is always painful and grieving is the way we face this deeply emotional experience.

As you realize how complicated grief is, the desire to transform this emotional pain into something good often emerges. The purpose of this book is to help you accomplish this goal.

First, a few words about the book itself: Throughout you will find questions that prompt you to think about your loved one and help you recall the things you want to remember about him or her. You will also find three appendices, one about the grieving process, another to write your thoughts about death, and a third containing useful information about the legal issues you will be facing. Beginning now, as you read further, make notes to yourself.

Creating Memories

WE REMEMBER THEM...

In the rising of the sun and in its going down,
   We remember them.
In the blowing of the wind and in the chill of winter,
   We remember them.
In the rebirth of spring,
   We remember them.
In the blueness of the sky and in the warmth of summer,
   We remember them.
In the beginning of the year and when it ends,
   We remember them.
When we are weary and in need of strength,
   We remember them.
When we are lost and sick at heart,
   We remember them.
When we have joys we yearn to share,
   We remember them.
So long as we live, they too shall love, for they are now part of us, as
   We remember them.

Jewish prayer for the dead

When we lose someone to death, we know our life has changed forever. From this moment forward there is no going back, starting over, or saying those things you forgot to say. There is only tomorrow, and you have this book in your hands because you want your tomorrows to include tangible memories of the person you loved.

We memorialize our loved ones in many ways — drawings, scrapbooks, quilts, donations to charity, and saving things that remind us of them. We can knit our way through grief, hike our way through it, and write about it. We do these things to help ourselves manage one of life's most painful experiences, to share memories that will help others remember too, and to keep someone we have loved alive in our hearts forever. This book uses the power of words, combined with photographs and whatever else you want to include, to help you record cherished memories of someone who helped make you who you are at this moment, and will remain a part of your life forever.

Writing to Remember...

Give sorrow words; the grief that does not speak
whispers the o'er-fraught heart and bids it break.

William Shakespeare — *Macbeth* IV.iii

Good grief, the kind that heals, is all about moving through the pain of loss and coming to rest in a place of gratitude for having shared our life with someone we have so dearly loved. Good grief allows peace to descend as it heals us. By finding ways to remain connected to our beloved through memories and new rituals that help us to remember, we gradually become whole again. Words are a very powerful means for achieving this goal, and we will help you use them to remember, and to heal.

Words can transform our lives, yet they are nothing more than tools used to convey meaning, and we choose certain words to express what we are thinking or feeling at any given time. Our words belong to us, and there is no right or wrong way to use them in remembering someone dear. It isn't even necessary to use whole sentences or correct grammar; instead think of your words as flowers you are planting in your healing garden, and select them for the memories you want to create. Don't be afraid of words; instead let your heart decide how you use them to say what you want to say, tell the story you want to tell, and create a portrait of the one you love. This is your story and no one can tell you how to write it, so think of our suggestions as just that — ideas to help you along the way as you design your garden.

Throughout the book you will find questions. These are guides for you if you need them, but if you don't, let your own vision take over.

Before you begin, spend a few moments thinking about your grief. Don't dismiss it as unimportant or self-indulgent, or try to make it go away. Invite it to be your best friend for a time and allow the feelings it engenders to guide you as you create your healing garden.

Become aware that you experience nearly everything first through your senses, and this is where memory arises. Get into the habit of paying attention to sensory clues that remind you of your beloved and choose words that describe what you saw, smelled, felt, heard, tasted, or otherwise reacted to. Pay attention to detail.

For example, what are some of the scents you remember? Is it a perfume or after shave lotion, or even the smell of a cigar or a cigarette?

Whenever I smell Old Spice I think of Dad...

Grandma poured lavender water over everything, including the houseplants. I sometimes wondered if she drank it too.

His breath always smelled like his favorite peanut butter and jelly sandwich.

What did your beloved feel like to you? Were their hands rough or soft? Were his muscles hard? Was her skin smooth?

Every ray of sunlight she ever caught shined on her face — and it was smooth as silk...

Nobody ever wondered if Granddad was a farmer after they shook his hand.

The baby felt so small in my arms.

What did his laugh sound like? Was his voice deep? Did she sing in the kitchen? Did he yell like a hog caller?

She could sing like an angel, except in church...

He snored like a buzz saw — and now that he's gone it's so quiet I can't sleep...

Whenever I heard a baby cry I always knew whether or not it was her.

Are there certain foods that you associate with this person? When you taste the garlic in spaghetti or see steak on a menu, does it remind you of a favorite meal you always ate together? When you see scrambled eggs do you remember how much he hated them?

I don't know how he got through life without ever eating a tomato — he hated them...

She never ate a hamburger because she thought eating a cow was no different from eating your best friend.

I never knew a kid who could eat so much macaroni and cheese at one time.

What did you see when you looked at this person you loved? Melancholy eyes or eyes that sparkled and danced; hair like a raven or bleached by the sun; a thin, angular face or a dimpled chin?

Sometimes his eyes were so dark I could see myself reflected back in them...

Her smile lit up the room — sometimes the whole house! And one stern look from her could bring us kids to our knees.

He was a whole bag of squirming giggles.

What about your beloved made you laugh? Caused you to cry? Angered you? Touched your soul? What about them do you love so much?

She wrecked more cars than any woman I ever knew — finally I just gave up being mad at her about it.

At least once a week he hoisted a few and promised to die for Ireland... claimed it was his patriotic duty.

She loved to play dress-up in my clothes, and wore my make-up like a clown.

The secret of finding your way through the healing garden is in the details that you create. These details form the picture of your beloved that ultimately leads you to know, in your heart, that you will remain connected forever.

Sense your grief and use words to bring your memories back to life. Know that sometimes this will be hard, and don't be afraid of your pain. Instead, use it to help you on your journey and guide your way as you create enduring memories that keep the circle of life alive and vibrant.

Remembering the Good...
Remembering the Bad

Every man hath a good and a bad angel attending on him in particular all his life long.

Robert Burton: *The Anatomy of Melancholy* I.ii.1.2

Love, no matter how deep, ebbs and flows and we have conflicts with everyone we love. Don't forget the hard parts of your relationship and don't shy away from critical comments. Your beloved was dear to you, but not perfect. Don't erase or smooth over the imperfections because they are as much a part of your beloved as all the endearing qualities, and to dismiss them is to create an incomplete picture of someone dear to you. The picture you create, just as death, must lie in the truth.

When he drank too much he could be foul mouthed and cruel.

Her anger would arise in a flash, out of nowhere, and she could hold a grudge for days.

He was the messiest kid alive, and we fought endlessly over cleaning up his bedroom.

Planting Your Garden of Memories

Now is the time for your journey to begin, and as you write think about the wonderful gift of memories you are creating for the family and the friends of your beloved, and for yourself.

Who was this person I loved so much?

**I love thee,
I love but thee,
With a love that shall not die till the sun grows cold,
And the stars are old,
And the leaves of the Judgment Book unfold!**

Bayard Taylor: *Bedouin Song*

This is where you tell your story about your beloved. Begin by writing his or her name and identifying your relationship to him or her and how long you shared part of your life with this person.

Next look at the obituary. Generally an obituary contains only the facts of a person's life, and sometimes we would like to say more. We would like to add something more personal. If you could say more about your loved one, what would you write? Think of phrases like:

She made the best banana cream pie.

He loved to fish for trout.

She read romance novels.

He read the Bible every evening.

He cooked pancakes for breakfast on Sunday mornings.

Place the newspaper obituary in this space and then add personal lines of your own about your loved one that were not included in the newspaper. This is a good place to note personal characteristics such as date of birth, place of birth, height, weight, hair color, left/right-handed, date of death, and place of death.

Describe the funeral (place, type of service, burial rites.) How did you say good-bye? Did something unexpected happen? Think about your beloved's favorite flowers. Is there anything you wish would have been different?

Now think about the life of the person you loved. Where did he/she attend school? What kind of work did he/she do? What were his/her favorite possessions (fishing poles, baseball cards, jewelry, teddy bear, soccer shirt) activities (sports, crafts, travel, movies) and pastimes? Where did he/she travel? What special moments do you remember? What special characteristics of your beloved come to mind (a smile that lit up a room, told awful jokes, always cried in sad movies?) What shape would this plot in your garden be?

How did family fit into your loved one's life? What role did he/she play in the family (caretaker, event organizer, black sheep, favorite son/daughter, athlete, scholar, jokester, etc.) what tree or flower best describes your beloved's family relationships? Is there an animal (birds, rabbits, puppy dog) that should be encouraged to inhabit this space in your garden?

What was your relationship to your beloved? What will you miss and what won't you miss at all? What special plans did you have? What special moments did you share together? What dreams died with your beloved? What activities and rituals did you share? What was life like with him/her? What flowers would the two of you have planted together every spring?

Relationships are reciprocal, and this book is helping you fully grasp what your loved one meant in your life. Spend a few minutes now considering what you imagine your loved one felt about you? Were you your father's or mother's only daughter or son? What did this mean to them? Were you your sibling's best friend? How did this friendship enrich their life? Were you your grandparent's first grandchild, your aunt or uncle's favorite niece or nephew? Were you your loved one's parent or life-long best friends with the one who has died? Did you know you were the great love of his (her) life? What do you suppose this gift meant to your beloved?

28

What aspects of your beloved's personality were really irritating? What did you argue about? What bad habits seemed impossible to break (cracking knuckles, chewing gum, spitting tobacco?) This is where you plant your favorite roses, remembering that the thorns are part of even the most beautiful rose bush.

Recall some of your favorite stories about your loved one — the "remember when..." ones that give a glimpse of your beloved's personality. When you think of him/her, do you think of daisies, sunflowers, vegetables, or thistles and weeds?

Reflect on the times when you both did things you wish you hadn't. What weeds in your garden would you like to pull up? What would you replace them with?

If your beloved were helping you write this book of memories, what would he/she want to be sure you said? Think about the happy times, the funny things he/she did, the simple kindnesses that held you together and that you will miss. This is where you plant your forget-me-nots.

No garden is complete without some trees. What trees remind you of your beloved — a weeping willow, a sturdy oak, a flowering magnolia, or a row of lilacs, wisteria vines, or night-blooming jasmine? This is where you describe what your beloved was most proud of, what he/she would want to be his/her enduring legacy.

The Future

We do best homage to our dead by living our lives fully even in the shadow of our loss.

– Jewish prayer

Grief lessens over time, and soon your thoughts will turn to how you want to fill the space created by the absence of this beloved person in your life. What ideas do you have about ways to honor this important person in some continuing way? What would you plant in this garden space? Some people plant trees, flowers, or establish memorials, scholarships, hold golf outings or other events.

If you were to write your beloved a letter telling him/her about your life with them, and now without them, what would you say? How would you describe the garden you have planted as you have endeavored to remember them?

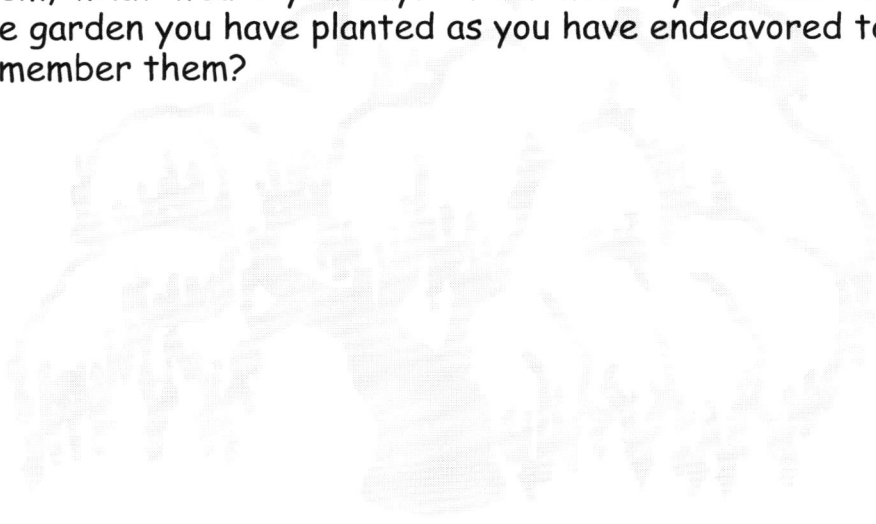

    What new rituals do you want to create to help you and others remember this person? How will the rain and sun shine upon his/her memory to keep it alive? Will you build a park bench in your backyard, engraving his/her name on it and sit there in the evenings? Will you make an annual trip to his/her favorite vacation place? Will you keep his/her ashes in a vase displayed in your home? Will you have a piece of his/her artwork displayed in your home? Will you place his/her photo in a frame and wake up in the morning and talk to it; or say good night to it as you go to bed? What unique things do you think would specifically help you remember his/her life?

Will the circle be unbroken by and by, Lord, by and by...
—American folk song

Mementoes

Memory can tell us only who we were in company of those we loved; it cannot help us find what each of us, alone, must now become. Yet no person is really alone; those who live no more echo still within our thoughts and words, and who they were has become woven into who we are.

– Jewish prayer

This is where you will insert anything you want to add to this garden — photos, poetry, news clippings, souvenirs, funeral memorabilia, and anything else that comes to mind to enrich the soil in your garden.

Bless the Lord, winter cold and summer heat...
Bless the Lord, dews and falling snow...
Bless the Lord, nights and days...
Bless the Lord, light and darkness...
Bless the Lord, ice and cold...
Bless the Lord, frosts and snows;
   Sing praise to Him and highly exalt Him forever.

Book of Daniel: 3:45-50

Appendices

I. The Grieving Process

The grieving process is extremely complex and can differ remarkably from one person to the next. Unfortunately, modern American culture generally fails to recognize that there is no right or wrong way to grieve and that the process takes as long as it takes. The tendency is to want to "grieve and move on" as quickly as possible. Within a few days of a funeral we are expected to "get back to normal," stop our public displays of sorrow, and start functioning again. Other cultures treat grief more gently, allowing for an extended period of intense mourning followed by a period of readjustment as we create a "new normal" following the loss of a loved one. This book hopes to give you permission to stop and grieve for a while, and while you are in this life space, create lasting memories of your loved one.

The journey through grief is uncharted, sometimes confusing, and often irrational. We want to know what will happen next and when the pain will end, and that answer is different for everyone. However, there is one guiding principle — your loss won't always hurt as much as it does now, but it will always hurt a little, and your life will never be the same. It will be a good life, but it will be a different life than it was when the person you loved was physically present in your life. Your task now is to begin creating your new life without forgetting the person that was so important to you in your old one. Your grief is an opportunity to begin writing a new chapter in your life story.

Grief is never something we choose — it is always imposed upon us. Consequently we feel out of control as the myriad of grief emotions move into our psyche, often overtaking us and stubbornly refusing to leave until we face them head on. Following are the most common emotions associated with grieving:

** Denial — it isn't really the longest river in the world, but it is perhaps the oldest one. Grief and denial go hand in hand. Denial tells us this really isn't happening, that nothing has really changed, that our dearly beloved isn't really gone and he or she will be coming back any minute. Our rational mind knows none of this is true, but our emotions claim otherwise. Early in the grieving process denial can protect us from the full impact of our loss until we are ready to handle it, but it's not a place where we want to spend an extended period of time.

** Numbness — Being numb, is a form of denial; it is being unable to feel anything and, like denial, can be protective up to a point. Numbness allows time to get used to what has happened on an intellectual level, and as it slowly dissipates we begin to feel our aching heart. As frightening as this may seem, think of it as the thawing out of frozen emotions that must occur before the river of life can begin flowing once again, and endeavor to be with the process of slowly beginning to feel once again.

** Anger — Anger is a natural reaction to being robbed, in this case, of someone we have loved dearly. We can be angry at God, the doctors who failed to cure or save the life of the one we loved, our friends and family who are still alive, angry at ourselves for what we did, or failed to do, and angry at the one who died. Sometimes we are simply angry at the world because our loss leaves us feeling powerless. Anger over the situation we now find ourselves in is normal, and there is no reason to feel ashamed or guilty when these feelings arise.

** Regret — When someone dear to us dies often we are thrust into a detailed examination of our relationship with that person. "I should have...

if only... what if... why didn't I..." occupy most of our vocabulary whenever we think about our life with this person, and pretty soon guilt moves into our head and dominates our grief. Guilt is not a welcome guest in our psyche and it is important not to allow it to become a permanent resident. Because we can't go back and redo our relationship with our beloved, avoid thoughts of "should have" and instead focus on what you can do now to remember this person lovingly and well.

** **Sadness** — Sadness comes in waves, and will continue to happen for a long time. Like waves crashing onto a beach, some are more intense than others, and so it is with periods of sadness. True sadness brings with it a haunting beauty that transforms as it cracks us wide open to life. Sadness is an important part of the grieving process, thus not to be avoided, because out of it comes the wisdom and understanding that softens us to life and enables us to gently create our new life apart from the one we love.

** **Acceptance** — Eventually, whether or not we actively choose it, we accept the loss of our loved one. We realize our life will never be the same, and that there is nothing we can do about this, so we give up wailing against the forces that caused this to happen to us and simply let go. We release our loved one to their new life and begin embracing our own, equipped with the wisdom we have gained through our grieving process.

All of these emotions can be experienced within a period of minutes, hours, or days, may be brief, or last a while, and they will come and go on their own timetable, for a long time. There is no formula or predictability to our feelings' appearance, reappearance, or disappearance from our conscious awareness. Grief isn't linear — it's a random and scattered emotional process that, if experienced with tender awareness, can transform us as we remember the one we love as the grace and blessing to us they were, and forever will be.

There is no grief which time does not lessen and soften.

Cicero: Epistolae IV.v.

II. Thoughts on Death

This existence of ours is as transient as autumn clouds. To watch the birth and death of beings is like looking at the movements of a dance. A lifetime is like a flash of lightening in the sky, rushing by like a torrent down a steep mountain.

—Buddha

It's often said that the only two certainties in life are death and taxes — and every death brings with it a tremendous loss for those who are left behind to grieve.

Your grief will be governed to a considerable extent by your beliefs around life, death and loss. It will be helpful to take some time to think about this death and what it means to you. There is space at the end of this journal to share these thoughts, if you want to. For now, just jot them down somewhere, and then revisit the questions when you have completed your journey through the healing garden.

Don't be afraid to cry, even if you are afraid that if you begin you'll never be able to stop. You won't go on crying forever, and when you do stop you'll feel as if a burden has been lifted and you are a little more light-hearted.

There is sacredness in tears. They are not the mark of weakness, but of power. They speak more eloquently than ten thousand tongues. They are messengers of overwhelming grief, of deep contrition, and of unspeakable love.

Washington Irving

Here are some questions about death to think about:

Do you view death as natural and just another point on the continuum of eternal life or view life as finite? Do you believe in a bodily resurrection or some other form of continuing life? Is death the final ending of life or a new beginning as life goes in a different direction from what it was on earth?

As you face the grief brought about by the loss of your loved one it is sometimes helpful to think about the death your loved one experienced. Was it an end to a difficult illness filled with suffering and pain or the result of a terrible tragedy that cut a promising life short?

How did death occur? Were you present at the time of death? If you were not, do you feel you should have been with the person? Would it have made a difference if you had been with your beloved at the time of their death?

Why did death occur now? Who else is sorry to have lost this person? Do you believe there were relatives waiting to welcome your beloved into the next life?

When sleep won't come what do you think about? How do you express your anger? In what ways do you want to let go, and in what ways do you want to remain connected to your beloved?

He lives, he wakes – 'tis Death is dead, not he.

Shelly: Adonais XLI

III. Helpful Information

One short sleep past, we wake eternally, and death shall be no more; death thou shalt die.

John Donne: Holy Sonnets

First, we extend our condolences to you on the loss of a loved one. For some of you, this loss is as close and personal as the loss of a spouse or a child. For others, it may be a more distant relative or a friend who held a special place in your heart and in your mind. For those of you where the loss may be an exceptionally close loss, there are a number of things that need to be done, or may be required to be done by you because of your relationship, and perhaps some of them mentioned in the following pages have already been accomplished. However, we would like to make some suggestions that, hopefully, will be helpful to you in determining what steps need to be taken when you have lost someone special in your life.

What happens upon the death of a special one in our lives? If death occurs at a hospital or a medical facility and a doctor is present, then the doctor will issue a death certificate. If the death occurs outside of a medical facility, such as a home or in an accident, then it is necessary to contact a physician or the coroner. Sometimes in the event of an accidental death, it may be necessary to have an autopsy performed. This is nothing more than the coroner trying to determine what the cause of the death may be. Do not be afraid of this. It's merely a procedure that is often required by law and is always done respectfully.

Depending upon your relationship with your loved one, you may be called upon to make decisions with regard to his/her body and estate. One of the first decisions that you will have to make is whether or not there should be a donation of body parts and tissues. This is something that most families talk about prior to death. If you haven't had this discussion you may want to locate estate planning documents to see if the deceased had expressed any desires with regard to this. Many times, authorization for donation of body parts is contained on a driver's license or on a card that may be regularly kept in a wallet.

Typically, the next step is to notify family and friends of the death. It is impossible for someone close to the deceased to sit down and notify all of the family and friends of a loved one. Do not try to do it. Try to look at the contact process as a tree with many branches. Contact one person on each one of these branches and advise them of the circumstances and ask them to follow through and to call the people along their branch. This will allow you to get the maximum number of people informed of the death, within a minimum amount of time. Your friends and relatives are suffering too, and allowing them to help out lessens their pain. If you are aware that there are a number of people that have not been contacted, look for a Christmas card list or other mailing list that might exist. After the funeral arrangements have been made, you may want to use this to contact out of state relatives and friends.

When notifying people about the death of a loved one, consider others that should have been notified. Typically, besides friends and relatives, all employers or other sources of income, including social security, should be notified. Additionally, if the individual had been a member of the armed forces, they may have certain death benefits that are available, and the armed forces should be contacted. The number for the Veteran's Administration is 1-800-827-1000, and if the decedent was a veteran, there may be certain benefits, including financial assistance and military funeral or some type of commemoration of his/her service to the country.

If there had been specific funeral or burial instructions left with an estate plan, then your job is much easier. If not, you should consult with other close family and friends to discuss funeral arrangements. If it's going to be a religious service, you should contact the rabbi, priest, pastor, minister or other religious leader for help in determining how the funeral should occur once the body has been taken to the funeral home. The funeral home director will usually help with burial or cremation arrangements and will be a great resource regarding the coming days. Generally funeral and burial arrangements will include decisions about services, cremation, viewing of the body, and other specifics that will help comply with instructions left by the decedent.

Usually an obituary runs in a local paper. Sometimes these are free and sometimes there's a cost. Most newspapers will help you prepare the obituary, but they will look to you for the information to be included. At a minimum, you should advise them of the date of the death, the location of the funeral service and whether or not there will be visitation. Typically, there is an indication of what lineal descendants are left behind and a brief mention of any prior employment and any associations the decedent may have had during their life.

Once you've gotten this far you need to step back, take a deep breath and reflect on whether the funeral and burial arrangements are completed as you wish them to be. If the decedent has left a house, make sure someone watches the house during the funeral itself. Unscrupulous people can take advantage of your loss by burglarizing a home based upon information that they have seen in the newspaper. Asking a neighbor to watch the house during the services will prevent even more heartbreak from occurring.

After the funeral has taken place it is necessary to start looking for documents to take care of what has been left behind. This is called the estate. Typically, the funeral director will help you obtain copies of the death certificate because it is used for many things. There will be a need for a death certificate for every policy of life insurance, one to give each financial institution, and for any stock brokerage accounts that your loved one may have. It is better to have more than less, since it is much easier to get them at the time of death. Typically a number of 5-10 death certificates are obtained.

Many times there is a question regarding who is to be in charge of the estate. Usually there is one person, called the personal representative or the executor, identified in a will whose job it is to settle the estate. However, if there is no will, any relative can usually step forward and begin the process once the family decides who is to serve as the executor or personal representative or in the case of a trust, who the successor trustee may be. This person is responsible for making sure that all the arrangements are made, signing for the funeral expenses, making sure that creditors are paid, assets are distributed, estate tax returns are filed and generally straightening out the affairs of the decedent. The personal representative or executor is never responsible for the debts of the decedent unless they specifically commit to pay for them individually.

This personal representative can be an individual, a combination of individuals, or can even be a corporate body such as a trust company. The personal representative takes the will and files it with the court. If there is no will, then an interested person asks that the court appoint them as the personal representative. This personal representative will receive letters testamentary or letters of domiciliary which are indications of the authority for the personal representative to act for the estate.

The necessary estate planning documents are most often found in a safe deposit box or in a desk in the decedent's house, and include a will (document in writing which distributes the assets upon death) or a trust that may have been created by the deceased to provide directions regarding any assets that may have been owned by the trust during his/her lifetime. This type of trust is called a Revocable Trust. The personal representative should be looking for any funeral and burial plans, instructions to be followed in the event of a death, any life insurance policies and any pension/retirement benefits. These items are usually found in desk drawers or metal boxes in the back of closets. The personal representative usually finds old tax returns that might show the identification of stocks and bonds that may be owned or bank accounts, as well as any divorce documentation or any pre-nuptial agreements. Typically it's not difficult to locate old bank statements, checkbooks, or similar documents along with titles to motor vehicles and documentation of any insurance policies, including health insurance. All of these documents are important and should be taken into safeguard by the personal representative.

Once a will is found or the relatives have decided who should be the person in charge, then the will should be taken to a lawyer and the probate process should be started. It is not necessary to go through a lawyer to do this, but it is oftentimes helpful in dealing with the court systems. The court will issue domiciliary letters of probate after a petition for a will or a petition to proceed without a will is presented to the court. This gives the individual the authority to be the personal representative or executor, and to act in all manners.

The personal representative should contact the Social Security Administration and any other government agencies or any other benefit program that the decedent might have been involved with at the time of his/her death. The general Social Security Administration number is 800-772-1213 or 800-325-0778. It is necessary to do that because the Social Security office needs to be advised promptly. Checks are no longer allowed in the month of the death, and there is typically a death benefit that is paid to a surviving spouse. If checks are issued to the decedent after the death and are cashed or direct deposited, the Social Security office looks upon this as a matter of fraud.

If there is any life insurance, you should contact the company and make arrangements for a proof of loss statement. This is a document that indicates the essentials of who died, when and where and requires you to furnish a death certificate. Once it is filed with the insurance company, most insurance companies will contact you to advise you as to whom the beneficiaries may be. If the beneficiaries are an estate, then the monies go directly to the personal representative to be placed in an estate account. If there are named beneficiaries, then it goes directly to those named beneficiaries. Many times, the insurance company will allow the beneficiaries or the estate to keep the monies on hand with the insurance company in an interest bearing account to allow the beneficiaries to pull the money out over the course of time. If this option is available, the beneficiaries should consider it since the interest rate given by insurance companies may be more advantageous than placing it in an ordinary bank account.

The personal representative has an obligation to open a bank account for the estate. The bank also requires that a federal identification number be obtained. This federal identification number can be obtained from the Internal Revenue Service. This also can be obtained through the assistance of an attorney or an accountant. This account should receive all receipts and make all disbursements with records kept of each transaction. In this manner, you are able to account properly for all of the assets of the decedent and any expenses that may be incurred.

With receipt of the letters of domiciliary, the personal representative is able to liquidate the estate. This includes the sale of any real estate, the cashing in of any stocks and bonds, and the assembly of monies that constitute the assets of the decedent. It is also the responsibility of the personal representative to pay any debts and expenses that exist and to have the taxes determined. It is necessary to file a personal income tax form for the months the decedent was alive during the year of his/her death. It is also necessary to file an estate tax return, even if it is only informational to indicate that there are no taxes due. Once that has been done the remaining assets are distributed among the heirs. A receipt is obtained from those individuals and is either filed with the court or kept with the records to show that the assets have been properly handled.

The personal representative should make sure that they have collected all of the benefits that may be available to the decedent. Many associations or fraternal organizations may have death benefits available, and a call should be made to determine whether or not these exist. Additionally, not only should the bank accounts be checked, but the bank should be contacted to determine whether or not there is a safe deposit box where any valuable items may have been kept.

If instead of a will, there was a living trust created, it becomes irrevocable at the time of death. In such a situation, it is necessary for the trustee to file a fiduciary income tax return and to follow through with the directions contained in the trust.

In some instances, when the decedent has left a minor child, there may be a need for a guardian of the estate and a guardian of the person. A guardian of the estate is someone who ensures that any assets that are supposed to go to the minor children will eventually go to them. Typically, this is someone who is nominated in a will or if there is no will, can be appointed by the court. The guardian of the person or the children is usually somebody that is nominated to take care of the children until they reach the age of majority. If there is no one appointed, then typically, a relative will step forward to volunteer to take care of the children.

One of the key things that the personal representative has to do is make decisions. They decide whether items need to be sold, how they are going to be sold and how soon assets will be distributed. Do not be afraid to take your time. Typically, the probate process will take six months to a year. Make sure that your decisions are the right decisions and that you consult the family members as much as possible. If they are in agreement, then the process is easy. If there are disagreements, then the personal representative has to make the decision but can take into the account the wishes of the heirs and family members. The personal representative has the final authority for making sure that everything is done, and they are the person who makes the final decisions, subject to a ruling by a court. If you don't feel like you want to take this position, you can always decline, and the court will either appoint professional help or, in the alternative, allow another family member to step forward.

Once all of these items have been taken care of, you will be left with a grieving period. This book is an attempt to help you through this time. It is meant to be a guide as well as a memorial to your loved one and the relationship that you had with them that other family members and heirs can look at again and again and remember how special this person was.

If, at any time you feel that your grief has interfered with your ability to enjoy life or you believe that your grief has been so deep and you are suffering so much and it has lasted an inordinate amount of time, please consider seeking qualified medical assistance. A trained grief counselor may assist you greatly as you progress through the grief process.

Our hope is that this book will assist you to grieve well.

Patient Trust

Above all, trust in the slow work of God.

We are quite naturally impatient in everything to reach the end without delay.

We should like to skip the intermediate stages.

We are impatient of being on the way to something unknown, something new.

And yet it is the law of all progress that it is made by passing through some stages of instability--and that it may take a very long time.

And so I think it is with you.

Your ideas mature gradually--let them grow, let them shape themselves, without undue haste.

Don't try to force them on, as though you could be today what time (that is to say, grace and circumstances acting on your own good will) will make of you tomorrow.

Only God could say what this new spirit gradually forming within you will be.

Give Our Lord the benefit of believing that his hand is leading you, and accept the anxiety of feeling yourself in suspense and incomplete.

–Pierre Teilhard de Chardin SJ

OTHER THOUGHTS, REFLECTIONS AND MEMORIES

PHOTOGRAPHS

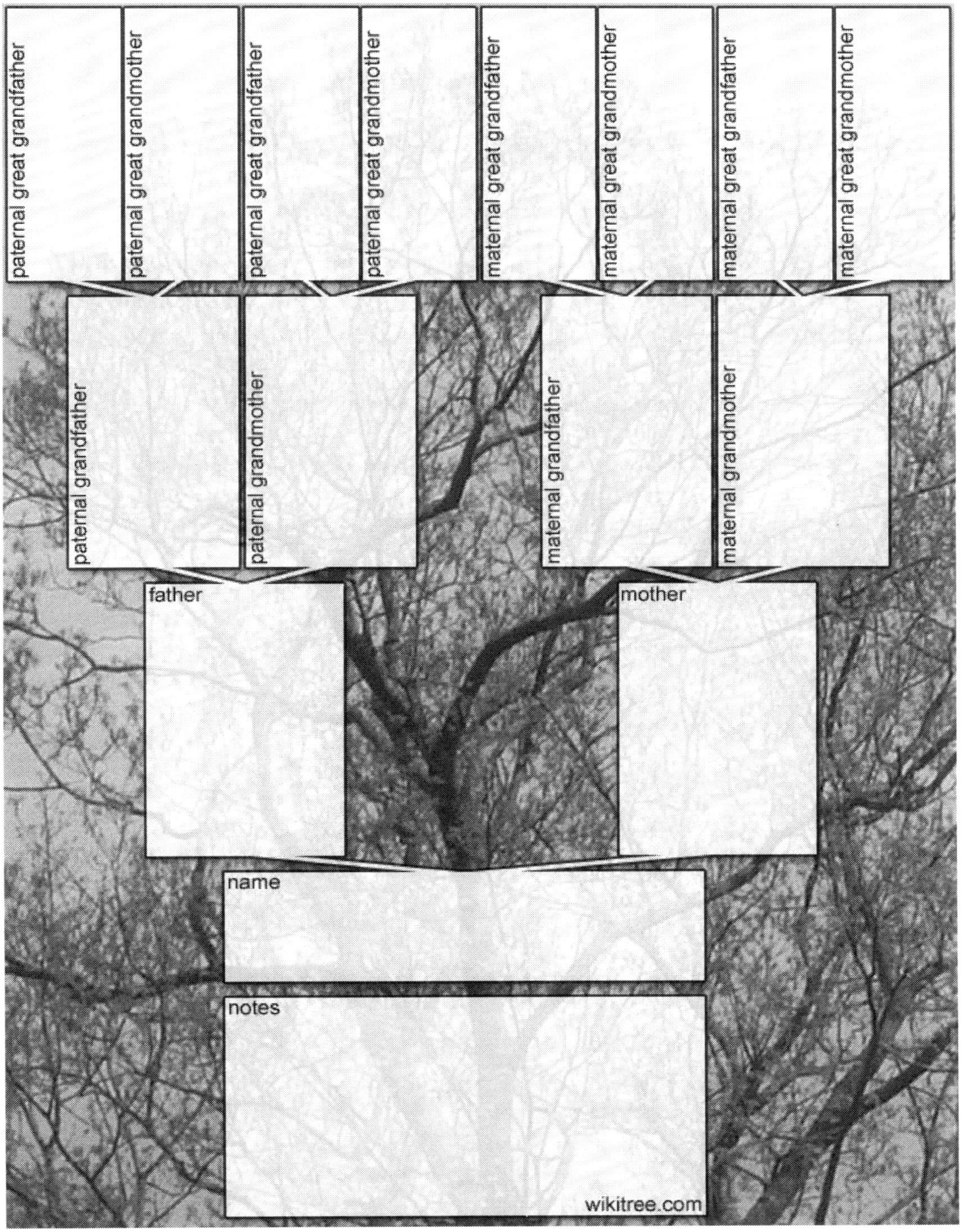

paternal great grandfather

paternal great grandmother

paternal great grandfather

paternal great grandmother

maternal great grandfather

maternal great grandmother

maternal great grandfather

maternal great grandmother

paternal grandfather

paternal grandmother

maternal grandfather

maternal grandmother

father

mother

name

notes

wikitree.com

Acknowledgements

We gratefully acknowledge the assistance of Deb Culhane and Rose Wolf, whose stellar formatting skills and meticulous proofreading abilities are unsurpassed. We also deeply appreciate Dr. Alice Thieman's thoughtful insights into the book's content. Each made a uniquely important contribution that allowed this book to become much more than it ever would have been without them. Their efforts immeasurably enrich the experiences each of you will have as you read and use this book to create lasting memories of a loved one that can be enjoyed by family members for generations to come.

To order additional books go to
www.memoriesofyoubook.com

Made in the USA
Las Vegas, NV
13 November 2021

34391014R00072